Ancient Kings
and Everyday Lessons

Ancient Kings
and Everyday Lessons

ALAN DODD

Foreword by Andrew Milne

RESOURCE *Publications* • Eugene, Oregon

ANCIENT KINGS AND EVERYDAY LESSONS

Resource Publications
An Imprint of Wipf and Stock Publishers
199 W. 8th Ave., Suite 3
Eugene, OR 97401

www.wipfandstock.com

PAPERBACK ISBN: 978-1-6667-3040-1
HARDCOVER ISBN: 978-1-6667-2191-1
EBOOK ISBN: 978-1-6667-2192-8

SEPTEMBER 20, 2021

To my family: my parents and my brother Ian,
and my wife Maya and children Greta and Jeremy.
Thank you for putting up with me over the years,
believing in me, and loving me. I love you too.

Contents

List of Tables/Illustrations

Foreword

Andy Milne

I FIRST MET ALAN some years ago when we both were in training as evangelists with Church Army UK, a missionary organization within the Anglican Church. I came to know him as someone with both a passion for Jesus and a passion to make Jesus known. Today, as an experienced and caring pastor, Alan is one with a desire to help ordinary people respond to God's call on their lives by learning to follow God's ways. Through this book, Alan fulfils that desire.

Ancient Kings and Everyday Lessons explores stories of both good and bad biblical kings. It helpfully investigates their lives, pulling out the positive and negative character attributes that show them as the characters they really were. Here we relive the lives of these ancient kings as they found themselves in positions of awesome human power but then had to contend with the issues of their people's disagreements, other nations' desires to conquer them, and of course, their own personal concerns.

As we turn the pages of this book, we go on a journey of exploration to see how these kings faced monumental challenges. Some turn to God and find help, flourishing as great examples to the people they lead, whereas others fall deeper into self and allow the flesh to get the upper hand. It struck me just how much they are like ordinary people living today. We find ourselves sympathizing with those weaker kings who are faced with struggles of temptation. We can stand in their shoes so to speak and wonder how we might react, and yet we're humbled to see how God uses such fallen people to be leaders of his people.

Alan makes many helpful connections with today's world so that whether you are a mum, dad, child, or grandparent, you can see how your own life can have a knock-on effect to those you love such as your own family. He also shows us the blessings and potential pitfalls to those who become leaders. Imagine a local shop manager, a mechanic with an assistant, a nurse with several trainees, a young leader, or a schoolteacher. Each has a level of influence on those with which they work. Here we find insights and pointers as to how we can discover more of God's help in our lives and learn to live in love for God and people.

The biblical kings' life stories are real and raw, there is no sanitized cover up. It's all visible and on show! As a result, we may see ourselves in some of their struggles as though God were holding up a mirror to our own inner thoughts and trials. May this cause us to draw near to the Creator and Savior of this world, asking his forgiveness when we fall short of his ways, receiving the Father's love afresh in our lives, and asking for strength to live like Jesus.

Acknowledgments

MY THANKS TO Paul Barnfield, Andrew Heron, and Paul Round who joined me in preaching the series on the kings of Israel at Hounslow Evangelical Church from which I took the inspiration to write this book.

Also, thanks must go to the church leadership, members, and congregation of Hounslow Evangelical Church for the space I have had to write this book and who encouraged my writing of it by their positive response to my preaching on the kings of Israel.

I give my thanks to Colin Bedford (now promoted to glory) who, through his faithful preaching from the Bible gave me both great knowledge and understanding but also a great desire to know it more and apply its truths to my life. I hope and trust that this book will give you, the reader, a similar desire to get to know God more through reading that far more wonderful book he has given us.

Lastly, but most importantly, I thank God for rescuing me from a life lived without him, and for paying for my wrongdoings in the death of my Savior and Lord Jesus Christ on the cross.

Introduction—The Kingdom of Israel

THE KINGS OF ISRAEL may seem like an irrelevant subject for today. They reigned around three thousand years ago in the Ancient Near East; a culture so different from our own. They existed in the Iron Age, long before the great cultural empires of the Greeks and the Romans. Yet, I hope this book will show you how the lessons of life discovered from their lives can be applied to our own, in the very different setting we find ourselves in and the very different status that we have (unless of course you happen to be a monarch!).

It is worth going back to the start so that we can consider how they came to reign there. The land of Israel was promised to the patriarch (and in effect the first Jew) Abraham around a thousand years earlier. The Bible verses containing these promises are found in the first chronological book of the Bible, the book of Genesis. Abraham believed God, and acted on God's command to him in trust and obedience. This is what God said when Abraham (or Abram as he was originally called) had traveled to Israel: "Then the Lord appeared to Abram and said, 'I will give this land to your descendants'" (Genesis 12:7a).

That promise held true although it took a long time to come to fruition. After about four hundred years in Egypt, much of it as slaves, the Israelites escaped their chains thanks to God's intervention and were free to enter the promised land. In a sad indication of things to come they disobeyed God, and it took another forty years until, under the leadership of Joshua, they went in, capturing the land from the peoples who were there. They had control of this land for the next four hundred years but continually forgot their commitment to God who had delivered them from their enemies. Consequently they lost God's protection, enemies attacked them, their crops failed or were stolen or damaged, and after a while they remembered God. In those times God raised up leaders known as judges who fought back against the enemies of the Jews and delivered peace. All was then quiet and peaceful for a while, until the people once again lapsed in their commitment to God and the cycle repeated itself. The final judge was a man called Samuel. He was also a prophet. While he was leading Israel the people came to Samuel and demanded he give them a king instead. The following, from 1 Samuel 8:6–18, is the account of what happened next:

> Samuel was displeased with their request and went to the LORD for guidance. "Do everything they say to you," the LORD replied, "for they are rejecting me, not you. They don't want me to be their king any longer. Ever since I brought them from Egypt they have continually abandoned me and followed other gods. And now they are giving you the same treatment. Do as they ask, but solemnly warn them about the way a king will reign over them."
>
> So Samuel passed on the Lord's warning to the people who were asking him for a king. "This is how a king will reign over you," Samuel said. "The king will draft your sons and assign them to his chariots and his charioteers, making them run before his chariots. Some will be generals and captains in his army, some will be forced to plow in his fields and harvest his crops, and some will make his weapons and chariot equipment. The king will take your daughters from you and force them to cook and bake and make perfumes for him. He will take away the best of your fields and vineyards and olive groves and give them to his own officials. He will take a tenth of your grain and your grape harvest and distribute it among his officers and attendants. He will take your male and female slaves and demand the finest of your cattle and donkeys for his own use. He will demand a tenth of your flocks, and you will be his slaves. When that

day comes, you will beg for relief from this king you are
demanding, but then the LORD will not help you."

Regardless, the people still wanted a king, and so Samuel was
sent away to anoint and prepare the first man for the job. But one
couldn't say the people hadn't been warned!!

The first three kings are not the subject of this book in any
great detail as I have decided to concentrate on the divided kingdoms which came later, but let me give a quick overview. Saul came
first, seemingly starting well, but he soon lost focus on God, went
his own way and was rejected by God before finally dying in battle.

God's appointed successor came from outside Saul's family
and indeed tribe. Thanks to Saul's turning away from God, David was actually anointed king while Saul was still alive and spent
the next two decades on the run. However, after Saul's death and
despite a desperate attempt from one of Saul's sons to keep the
throne, David was the obvious choice as king. David quickly established Jerusalem as his capital (after first taking it by force from
the previous occupants the Jebusites), and also the place where the
vitally important ark of the covenant would be kept. The ark of the
covenant contained the tablets of the ten commandments given to
Moses on Mount Sinai and was the most holy thing in all of Israel
as it was declared God's dwelling place on earth. David had many
faults, not least of which were pride, lust, and poor parenting skills,
but yet God's favor was on him as he kept on turning back to God
and yearning for God's name to be glorified.

After another inevitable power struggle, David's chosen successor, his son Solomon, took the throne. He had the fortune to
inherit a very large, wealthy, and peaceful kingdom thanks to his
father's successful military campaigns. Solomon had the honour of
building a more suitable structure to hold the ark of the covenant,
the great temple of Jerusalem. It was here that the Jews worshiped
and sacrificed. It was the focal point of their country and their religion. Solomon began his reign well, famously asking for wisdom
to govern his people when God offered him anything he wanted.
However, Solomon eventually went away from his commitment
to God, committing the crime of worshiping other gods. It seems

he went astray after marrying every woman he ever set eyes on. If you don't believe that claim, check out 1 Kings 11:1–3: "Now King Solomon loved many foreign women. Besides Pharaoh's daughter, he married women from Moab, Ammon, Edom, Sidon, and from among the Hittites. The Lord had clearly instructed the people of Israel, 'You must not marry them, because they will turn your hearts to their gods.' Yet Solomon insisted on loving them anyway. He had 700 wives of royal birth and 300 concubines. And in fact, they did turn his heart away from the Lord."

Solomon had inherited great blessings from his faithful father, but thanks to his moral and spiritual failures he would be storing up trouble for his sons and heirs.

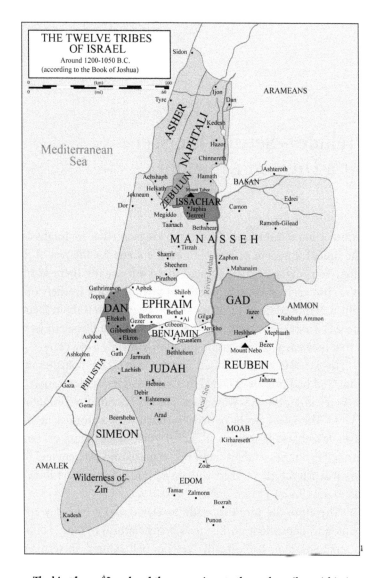

The kingdom of Israel and the areas given to the twelve tribes within it.

Prelude—Setting the Scene for a Divided Kingdom

I GAVE A BRIEF overview of the three kings of what we might call "the united kingdom of Israel" to set the scene for the rest of the book. You might be disappointed that I am leaving them at this point, but each of them is worthy of a whole book in their own right, and indeed many great books have been written about them.[2] There is a sort of symmetry to their reigns on the throne of Israel in that they each led the nation for approximately forty years.

In 931 BC Solomon died and his son Rehoboam became king. God had promised David that his lineage would last forever. However in Psalm 132, which was probably written by Solomon, it says: "The LORD swore an oath to David with a promise he will never take back. 'I will place one of your descendants on your throne. If your descendants obey the terms of my covenant and the laws that I teach them, then your royal line will continue forever and ever'" (Psalm 132:11–12).

Therefore the promise made to David was a two way covenant, and dependent on his heirs being faithful to God. Unfortunately Solomon had already "set the ball rolling" in terms of his own waywardness. In 1 Kings 11:9–13 we see judgment was already on his family:

---

2. For an interesting take on events during Saul's time as king and David's time as king, the historical novels written by Jill Francis Hudson are well worth a look. *Rabshakeh* covers the time of Saul and *Zoheleth* the time of David.

The LORD was very angry with Solomon, for his heart had turned away from the LORD, the God of Israel, who had appeared to him twice. He had warned Solomon specifically about worshiping other gods, but Solomon did not listen to the LORD's command. So now the LORD said to him, "Since you have not kept my covenant and have disobeyed my decrees, I will surely tear the kingdom away from you and give it to one of your servants. But for the sake of your father, David, I will not do this while you are still alive. I will take the kingdom away from your son. And even so, I will not take away the entire kingdom; I will let him be king of one tribe, for the sake of my servant David and for the sake of Jerusalem, my chosen city."

The following kings, of whom this book is about, reigned over two areas of Israel which became separated. It is clear from the beginning that this was not ideal or desirable for a people who were supposed to reflect the God they were created to worship. The biblical books detailing their lives are 1 and 2 Kings (referred to in 1 and 2 Chronicles as "The Commentary of the Book of the Kings") and 2 Chronicles (referred to in 1 and 2 Kings as "The Book of the History of the Kings of Judah"), and differ at times in content and emphasis. Without making this book into a historical study I will attempt to reconcile the differences in the accounts. One major difference is that 2 Chronicles is more concerned with the southern kingdom of Judah and the progression of the Davidic line and often ignores the northern kingdom unless it directly affects Judah.

The following chapters are based loosely on the content of a series of talks given at Hounslow Evangelical Church, UK, from January to April 2015. I gave the majority of these talks, but for three of the kings I have used material from other speakers with their permission, and this is acknowledged at the end of each relevant chapter. As you read these chapters, you will notice that there are frequent Bible references, and you might well want to have a Bible available, so that you can read these and their context. If you would prefer to read an electronic version, Bible Gateway (www.

biblegateway.com) has a great selection of Bible translations, and you are welcome to use whichever you prefer. However, for your reference I have quoted from the New Living Translation (unless indicated otherwise).

Let's now turn to the rise of the kings of the divided kingdom.

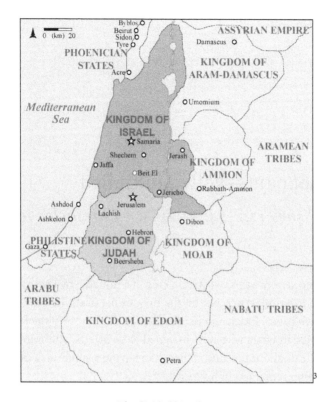

The divided kingdom.

1

Rehoboam—Folly Multiplied

1 Kings 12:1–24; 14:21–3; 2 Chronicles 10–11

REHOBOAM STARTED OFF AS the king of a united Israel with all the twelve tribes together, but by the time of his death he only ruled over two tribes, Judah and Benjamin, as well as those of the Levites (the tribe in Israel who were assigned to be priests, and were scattered throughout the land rather than having a single area of their own) who remained in his territory.

Rehoboam in many ways inherited a bad hand from his father Solomon. For one, he seemed to inherit Solomon's idolatry, that is his worship of other gods, which was always going to bring judgment from the one true living God. God does not allow worship to be shared. Worship is for him alone. Consider Exodus 20:2–5a, with the first two of the ten commandments which form the bedrock of the law given to the people of Israel:

> I am the LORD your God, who rescued you from the land of Egypt, the place of your slavery. You must not have any other god but me. You must not make for yourself an idol of any kind or an image of anything in the heavens or on the earth or in the sea. You must not bow down to them or worship them, for I, the LORD your God, am a

jealous God who will not tolerate your affection for any other gods.

It is not enough to worship God and a whole host of other gods or idols. God has no rivals or worthy adversaries or competitors. He alone is Lord, and he alone created the universe and all that is in it, speaking the word and giving life and form to all things (see Genesis 1). As the book of Deuteronomy tells us: "He alone is your God, the only one who is worthy of your praise" (Deuteronomy 10:21a).

Rehoboam was given a test early in his kingship. It called on him to act humbly with regard to his people. He needed to borrow an early principle from Solomon's life which was to ask God for help in leading his people, and in desiring the best for them. Solomon, by all accounts, had lost this humility by the end of his reign, and Rehoboam was about to make the same mistake.

First Kings 12:1–24 details the showdown between Rehoboam and the rebel Jeroboam. It is interesting that Rehoboam would go to Shechem in the north of the country to be crowned king. It would surely have made more sense to be crowned king in his capital and hometown Jerusalem. Instead he made the journey into an area of the land which was less well disposed to him.

It is worth saying at this point that Rehoboam was used to luxury, used to everyone obeying his every command, and he probably couldn't comprehend the fact that he might not be universally popular. He was very much out of touch with public feeling.

While he was there, the people, led by Jeroboam, insisted that Rehoboam relax the tax burdens and labor demands on the people. They even promised loyalty if he would compromise, perhaps scale back a little on his luxury, tighten the royal belt a bit so to speak. His first response to this is admittedly a wise one. He asks for time to think about their demands. For three days he consults with his advisers. The older advisers who had also served his father Solomon suggested he agree to the people's request. There was a great residual loyalty to the king and the royal establishment. Although Solomon had damaged the relationship between king and people due to his onerous demands on them, it was repairable.

At this point Rehoboam could have made another wise choice. But he had friends in his peer group (probably the other rich entitled kids he had played with and learned with when he was growing up) that he also looked to for advice. These people knew how to ingratiate themselves with the king, and what would work in massaging his ego and in turn get them further recognition and reward. They decided to appeal to Rehoboam's pride and the entitlement that came with royal status. There was also the added temptation for him to step out of the shadow of David and Solomon and make a name for himself. So the advice was to not give in to the people's demands but instead to crack down on any dissent. Rehoboam sadly took that advice, and the kingdom's split was confirmed. He is quite well known compared to some of the other kings in this book, but his main claim to fame is for being the man who saw the dividing up of the kingdom of Israel on his watch. Not a good legacy at all.

The only wise move he made (apart from asking for three days' thinking time) was that, after the shock of hearing about the murder of the man he sent to restore order in the north of Israel, he fled back to Jerusalem and then thought better of mobilizing forces against Jeroboam and the ten tribes, having finally listened to a prophet sent by God (see 1 Kings 12:18–24). In avoiding that futile war, he did at least save the territory he did have. He was in fact spared to reign for seventeen years in total, although in the latter part of his rule he was effectively made subject to the Egyptian king Shishak who attacked Judah and ransacked Jerusalem, and only again avoided complete destruction when he humbled himself before God after being warned by the same prophet he had heeded earlier (see 2 Chronicles 12:1–12).

Throughout this story we see God working behind the scenes. In the judgment that was forewarned in Solomon's time, Rehoboam is permitted the folly of hitting the self-destruct button on his kingdom. If he had stayed loyal to God, the Lord would have postponed the judgment till after his time as king. However, in Rehoboam's time the idolatry in the land got worse (see 1 Kings 14:22–24), and he himself is condemned by these words in 2

Chronicles 12:14: "But he was an evil king, for he did not seek the LORD with all his heart." He also acted with great folly; I suspect not self-destructing completely only because God was protecting the family line of David from annihilation.

TO THINK ABOUT

David was not perfect by any means, yet he was willing to learn from his mistakes. He was thus able to give his son Solomon a good start to his reign as king. Solomon on the other hand squandered the blessings God gave him, and left the country in a mess (basically a powder keg of discontent and anger which would explode unless handled carefully).

If you are a parent, take time out to consider the legacy you are leaving your children. I don't mean in terms of financial wealth, but with regard to the example you are setting them in your character, your response to the curveballs life throws at you, your attitude to God not just in your words but in your actions, and the way you treat other people, particularly those who are vulnerable or lowly. Is the example you set one you can be proud of, and one which will mold your children into being kind and considerate? Does it point them toward God? Or is the example you set one which you are ashamed to think about? It might be too late to repair some damage, but it is certainly not too late to change course and ask God for help in rebuilding your relationship with, and your reputation in the eyes of, your children.

Another question is this: Are you out of touch with your children? Do you have any idea how they are feeling or the situations they might be going through? I know teenagers particularly are often evasive, being reluctant to let their parents in to their lives, but parents must be ready and willing to be there to listen when their son or daughter needs them.

It is a certain truth that actions have consequences. For these kings they were particularly far-reaching because of the responsibility they had, and the power and influence they wielded. Rehoboam did inherit a bad hand, but if he had acted wisely, put his trust in God alone, and above all humbled himself, there would have been a different outcome of his reign as king. We may ourselves have inherited a bad hand, a set of circumstances in our lives that are not the best. However, God can redeem them, and he can help us through them, but we need to trust him, obey him, and be willing to walk the path of life he has set for us.

Then there is the whole matter of advice. It is generally a good thing to ask people for advice when considering a difficult matter in our lives. Some people go too far with this, and ask just about everyone they see for their input into a situation. They usually do this because they are shopping around until they find someone who says what they want to hear, at which point they will happily take that advice. Rehoboam sought a second opinion on a situation which would break up an entire country, and because it pleased him to hear it, he followed it, and the result was devastating. We should always consider who we are speaking to, what their experience is in the subject we are talking about, whether they have an impartial or unbalanced perspective, and what motives they may have in giving us one piece of advice or another. Once we have received the advice, we need to pray it through, offering it to God, and then make the decision we believe is right. It is always worth considering unwelcome advice, rather than rejecting it simply because we don't like it.

Finally, we need to think about what it takes for us to move away from a destructive attitude or direction in our lives. Pride is dangerous as it prevents us from being willing and ready to change tack. Men especially are notoriously unwilling to turn their car around when going in the wrong direction, and this can easily transfer over to life as a whole. Rehoboam was in the end willing to resign himself to changing course, and it saved him from complete destruction. However, it was rather late when he did so, and he had to put up with severe consequences for his sinful and rebellious actions. A challenge for each of us is to identify where we are going wrong and take steps to put things right or change direction before things get worse and the consequences for us become more far-reaching.

2

Jeroboam—An Opportunity Missed

1 Kings 11:26–40; 12:25—14:20

JEROBOAM WAS VERY MUCH God's man who was chosen to, in effect, punish Solomon for his turning to other gods, and Rehoboam for his continued foolishness and non-worship of God. God spared Jeroboam from Solomon's anger when he first started murmurings of discontent during his reign, and Jeroboam was able to escape to the safety of Egypt. He returned at the opportune moment of Solomon's death, and managed to turn ten of the tribes against the new king Rehoboam.

Jeroboam was successful in his rebellion and so began to reign as the first king of the northern kingdom of Israel. He was the first in a new dynasty, and one which of course was independent of David's lineage. In some ways, he is the most notable of all the kings we will look at in this book as he effectively founded a new nation. Among all the kings who ever reigned in the promised land of Israel, only he did this. Even the first king of the united nation, Saul, inherited a country from his predecessors as rulers, the judges. Rehoboam also presided over a new nation, but first it was the smaller southern kingdom, and second it was much diminished compared to what he had inherited. He effectively lost the majority of his land, the majority of the tribes, and the majority of his influence.

Jeroboam was the figurehead at the helm of the beginning of a powerful breakaway state, and great opportunities were there to be taken. However, almost immediately after he was installed as king in his new capital of Shechem, Jeroboam turned irrevocably away from the God of his people. Jeroboam must surely have remembered the words given to him by the prophet Ahijah, telling him that he would be king under the orders and providence of God. Ahijah's words to Jeroboam also included a promise that if he would only be obedient to God his dynasty would be established and blessed by God in a similar way David's had been. Instead of turning to God, and going to him for guidance, Jeroboam went for worldly wisdom. Jeroboam decided to set up idols in his new country as a means of controlling his subjects. He saw the worship of God in Jerusalem as a threat to his position and the new country itself. He set up altars to a Canaanite god called Baal, a fertility god. He attempted to combine it with a facade of worship to the God of Israel, but as we have already seen with Solomon in the introduction to this book, God will not be mocked with half-worship and will not put up with a hybrid religious observance which also worships others. As it happened, according to 2 Chronicles chapter 11 many of the Levites in the north of Israel abandoned Jeroboam's new kingdom and moved to Judah, so his faithless plans actually backfired badly.

Jeroboam's card was marked from that point on, and his dynasty's and his own destruction was set. Many years later, Jeroboam belatedly turned again to the prophet Ahijah for advice. He only resorted to going back to him because a tragedy had befallen his family. Jeroboam's son was dying and he hoped that perhaps Ahijah could do something about it. However, it was far too late then, both for Jeroboam's son's survival, and his legacy and family dynasty.

Although Jeroboam reigned for a good innings—twenty-two years—and actually outlived both Rehoboam and his son Abijam, his reign went downhill from that point. It was an opportunity missed; he blew his big chance. At first he had everything in his favor, and it looked as if he might bring the southern kingdom to its knees. However, by the latter years of his reign he had lost his son to an early death and he had been humiliated in a battle with Abijam of Judah, a battle his army would have surely won if God had not intervened against them. My guess is Jeroboam died a disappointed, bitter, and unfulfilled man. He promised so much, was obviously (in human terms) a gifted and talented leader, but his desire to go his own way and hold on to power in his own strength and wisdom brought about his demise.

TO THINK ABOUT

Here we see the corrupting nature of power. Jeroboam seemed only too willing to listen to the prophet when he told him good things were going to happen to him, and in order to gain power, but once he had got hold of that power he was less compliant. First Kings 13 accounts of a prophet who rebuked and condemned Jeroboam for setting up and participating in idol worship. Jeroboam's response was to attempt to seize him. However, instead Jeroboam was immediately punished by God as his arm withered. In panic he asked the prophet to seek God's healing for him, which surprisingly was granted (evidence of God's undeserved grace), but Jeroboam didn't learn his lesson or show due and lasting gratitude. Power had damaged him as a person and had irrevocably broken his relationship with God. He put his calling and his reign over the tribes as his highest priority and was not willing to risk that even for doing what was right in God's sight.

Let's be aware of the old adage that "power corrupts and absolute power corrupts absolutely." We must pray for our leaders, whether secular as in the government or heads of major companies, or religious as in large church and denominational leaders, that they are kept from simply serving themselves and their own interests. We must also pray that Christian leaders remember that their first calling is to obedience to God.

Similarly, it is important to remember that our calling into whatever job, vocation, or position we hold is secondary to our calling into God's kingdom as his sons, daughters, and co-heirs. We must not let our position in the workplace or our place in society define who we are. Too many people, including church leaders, have fallen into the trap of putting their position above all else, and it has become a source of pride and value for them. This can lead to one and usually both of the following:

- A leader whose main interest becomes to hold on to their position, resulting in becoming too authoritarian.

- A leader who considers themselves a failure because their work is going badly, or they have had to give it up and cannot get over this disappointment.

The antidote to both errors is of course to remember that what we have comes from the Lord, including our calling and our gifts and talents, and also to remember that we are loved by him not because of what we can do but because he has chosen to love us. We need simply to accept his grace and goodness, and to submit ourselves to his Lordship.

Jeroboam only turned back to God when things had got very bad. In fact, it was too little too late, and not even sincere, as it was purely driven by desperation. Do you turn to God only in desperate times? How stubborn are you with regard to the path you are walking on? Can I suggest that you commit yourself to God in all times, coming under his authority and seeking his leading.

Jeroboam became king and then immediately made an effective declaration of independence from following God. When we have success it is a time when we feel great blessing, yes, but also there is potentially great danger. To stand firm in our faith and not get proud or arrogant is a big battle we must win at that time. How many people who have declared their faith in God in their younger years, have had their heads turned by fame and fortune? There is a great list of people who have fallen foul of the trappings of the seductive pull of popularity, wealth, and stardom. For example Britney Spears was proud of her faith in Jesus when she first came on the scene as a singer. However, it did not take long for her to be pulled away from this, and to go down a different path. Going back a couple of generations, if you have ever heard Elvis Presley's gospel music, you will surely be struck by the passion and seeming genuineness (only he will have known how genuine) of his singing these praise songs for the Lord. Yet fame and fortune took him down a dark path, and we can only hope he made peace with God before his untimely death.

We shouldn't despise life's blessings and pleasures, but neither should we idolize them or hold them too tightly. It is only in God that we have our eternal identity, an everlasting hope, and a never-ending inheritance.[1]

1. Some excerpts from a talk given by Andrew Heron at Hounslow Evangelical Church on the 18 January 2015 have been used in this chapter. My thanks to Andrew for his permission to use the talk he gave for this purpose.

3

Abijam and Asa—
Bold Words, Wavering Actions

1 Kings 15:1–24; 2 Chronicles 13–16

ABIJAM

ABIJAM (HIS NAME IN 1 Kings) was also known as Abijah (in the 2 Chronicles account). He was the son of Rehoboam and was the first of the kings who inherited the much-reduced kingdom of Judah. If you take a look at the biblical accounts you will see that 2 Chronicles and 1 Kings have very different takes on Abijam. In 1 Kings he is written off as a wicked king who turned away from God and followed in the wayward footsteps of his father Rehoboam. In the account in 2 Chronicles he is painted in a far better light. He only reigned for three years, and his time as king was dominated by wars between his kingdom and the breakaway northern kingdom still led by Jeroboam. The apparent contradictions in the two accounts can be accounted for by the fact that Abijam may have simply made godly statements to impress the priests and other God-fearing citizens of his nation.

In 2 Chronicles Abijam warns the northern kingdom army and Jeroboam himself that they are foolish to think that they can fight against the kingdom of the Lord that is led by the descendants of David. He is proved correct, and despite having a smaller army his troops win a great victory and Jeroboam is sent home with a much-reduced army and reputation. However, the Bible is also clear that Abijam's deliverance is purely down to God's grace and his promises to Abijam's great grandfather David.

It appears that Abijam was someone who talked the talk but didn't walk the walk. He was one of those people who seemed to have all the right answers, but his life and actions didn't measure up, in fact they contradicted all his noble words. He appears to have been a bit like some US politicians in election year. Faced with an electorate with a large percentage of Christians, some may talk up their religious credentials, their faith, and even their relationship with God, when the reality is, I fear, rather different. Likewise with Abijam. His words sounded good, and carried a lot of truth, but did he really believe them himself or was he simply playing to the audience and whipping up religious and nationalistic fervor? The account in 1 Kings suggests that was exactly what he was doing.

ASA

Asa, on the other hand, is recorded in both 1 Kings and 2 Chronicles as a godly king. He was not without his mistakes, however, and interestingly 2 Chronicles is slightly more condemning of his actions than the account in 1 Kings, which is the opposite of the slant on Abijam's life.

Asa reigned for a long time—forty-one years—which was about the same length of time as the great kings Saul, Solomon, and David. He reversed some of the idolatry in the land which had been practiced under the reigns of Rehoboam and Abijam, and had sadly had its root during Solomon's time. He also removed the queen mother Maacah (who was actually his grandmother, the wife of Rehoboam) from her position of influence because she was encouraging idol worship.

The Lord did great things through Asa, giving him military victories and peace for his land, including a very impressive defeat of a large Ethiopian army.[1] Asa also had the benefit of a prophecy given to him by the prophet Azariah: "'Listen to me, Asa!' he shouted. 'Listen, all you people of Judah and Benjamin! The LORD will stay with you as long as you stay with him! Whenever you seek him, you will find him. But if you abandon him, he will abandon you'" (2 Chr 15:2). This prompted Asa to step up his religious reforms, and lots of God-fearing people from the northern tribes defected to Judah. However, years later, despite having seen God's hand at work on numerous occasions, Asa took fright when Baasha king of Israel effectively put an embargo on his land. Instead of asking the LORD for help, and trusting that he would deliver his land, Asa chose instead to rely on Ben-hadad the king of Syria. Ben-hadad did indeed help him out, and Judah was saved from economic destruction, but of course Asa and Judah were now in Syria's debt. When challenged on this by the seer Hanani (see 2 Chronicles 16:7) Asa lost his temper and put him in prison, and his reign ended badly with him mistreating the people and refusing to seek the LORD even when he became ill.

TO THINK ABOUT

Abijam was undoubtedly used by God. God even blessed the nation of Judah through him, enabling them to win a decisive battle over Jeroboam's northern kingdom. He stirred up the people in their faith in the God of Israel, and this was to their benefit. However, a reading of his personal life and faith suggests that he was only paying lip service to God. He didn't really follow the Lord or his teachings, and was more prone to worshiping the idols of the land. This speaks to me of national leaders who desire the Christian vote but are only playing out their faith. I mentioned US politics as being particularly susceptible to this shallow allegiance to God. As I write this, Donald Trump has recently come to the

1. Ethiopia in biblical times wasn't the modern state of Ethiopia, but was a kingdom which approximated to an area which today is northern Sudan and southern Egypt.

end of his time as the president of the US. In my opinion he has shown little sign, particularly in his lifestyle and manner, of being a committed believer in Christ. Yet many would argue that he has been used by God to stand up for Christians, and for me this is an example (like Abijam) of God using someone who is not necessarily godly to further his purposes.

The book of 2 Chronicles ends with a statement after both kingdoms in Israel had been destroyed, that Judah would eventually be allowed to return from its exile and rebuild the temple in Jerusalem (see 2 Chronicles 36:22–23). The leader who gave that permission was King Cyrus of the Persian empire. He realized he was acting under the authority of the God of Israel, yet there is no evidence that he actually turned from the gods of his nation to serve the living God. But he was even used by God in this way.

Similarly, we have the whole matter of compromise, of which it seems Asa, but particularly Abijam, were guilty. Compromise is often all too easy. It is what society, our families, our friends, our employers may want to push us into. There are times when compromise is both necessary and right. For example, a very unhappy marriage will result if neither partner compromises, and a very abusive marriage will result if one partner refuses ever to compromise, as it will mean the other always gives in. Compromise is also necessary to avoid all sorts of breakdowns even at a national level. A refusal to compromise could lead (and has often led) to wars breaking out. However, we must resist compromise when it comes to our faith. God calls for our absolute loyalty, after all he gave his only Son that we might have life. The Jewish leaders told Peter and John that they should compromise and speak of Jesus no more. Their response was unequivocal: "Do you think God wants us to obey you rather than him? We cannot stop telling about everything we have seen and heard" (Acts 4:19b–20). Likewise, we need to be wholehearted in our commitment to our Lord, putting him first, even if that means making painful or even dangerous decisions.

There is a challenge here for us. Are we seen as those who will vociferously stand up for God and our faith in him, but when it comes to living it out be sadly found wanting, to such an extent that even to non-Christians the discrepancy is obvious? This tendency to hypocrisy, and a disconnect between our words (claims) and our actions, is a bad witness and something we may need to say sorry to God for and commit ourselves to putting right. Preachers are particularly at risk of being guilty of a "Do as I say not as I do" attitude, whether consciously or unconsciously.

Asa was seen as a good king, however, at some point in his life he stopped trusting in God. He reminds me a bit of Solomon who started so well, but went off the rails. We don't know why this happened as, unlike Solomon, he isn't recorded as having worshiped idols or being turned away from his faith in God by his wives or any other influences. But Asa is still a reminder to us that it is easy for our faith to slip slowly away. We may get out of the habit of seeking and waiting on God in prayer. We might simply get disillusioned by the constant battles (whether spiritual, emotional, or in Asa's case literal physical ones). It seems the threat on Asa's land from Baasha of Israel's embargo was a turning point for bad. For whatever reason, and in spite of the clear deliverance God had already provided in Asa's life, he decided he wouldn't or couldn't trust God, instead turning to human sources (in this case Ben-hadad of Syria). He then compounded his error by punishing the messenger who rebuked him on God's behalf. Asa is just one in a long list of kings who started off serving God but then almost seemed to forget that God had been with them. He made the mistake of trusting in the protection of a foreign power, when he had already proven faithful and already seen God work miraculously.

Asa and others (for example Joash, Amaziah, and Uzziah) were guilty of forgetting God's past goodness to them. I believe this is why so many of the Psalms (the hymn book of the Jewish people) are focused on recounting God's past help to Israel. They constantly needed reminding of what God had done for them. It is why it is also so important that one of the marks of our faith is that we give thanks to God regularly. Thanksgiving is a vital aspect of our prayer life, and it should be something we practice intentionally, otherwise we can so easily forget the good times and bemoan our current state, particularly when life is difficult, tragedy strikes, or we face a dangerous situation. Paul and Silas gave thanks to God even while they were in prison having been whipped for preaching about Jesus (see Acts 16:22–32). They chose gratitude, and it changed their mindset, leading to an awesome deliverance from danger and the opportunity to tell the jailer about their faith in Jesus.

4

Ahab—Absolute Infamy

1 Kings 16:29—22:40; 2 Chronicles 18

AHAB IS PROBABLY THE most notorious king in Israel's history, and certainly of the northern kingdom (and yet there is a king of Judah who we will meet later who will give him a run for his money!). As you can see from the Bible passages above, Ahab has a lot written about him in the Bible. Ahab was of the house of Omri (his father), and his twenty-two-year reign was a period of stability in the northern kingdom of Israel after a series of coups, very short reigns, and bloodletting. His reign was relatively prosperous and his country influential. He inherited a strong and successful kingdom from his father centered on the new and most long-lasting capital of Samaria.

In many ways Ahab was a notable king, but sadly in the Bible it is for all the wrong reasons. In his reign the unthinkable happened. Jericho was rebuilt in absolute defiance of a curse made by the great Israelite leader Joshua after it was destroyed when the Jews conquered the land (see Joshua 6:26). As the first city conquered by the Israelites on their taking of the land of Canaan it was to be left desolate as a memorial to what had happened. Ahab ordered, allowed, or at least did nothing to stop, a man called Hiel rebuilding the city. Hiel did so at the expense of his firstborn and youngest sons' lives, in accordance with Joshua's curse many centuries before.

Ahab got into the sort of idolatry his predecessors as kings had been into. However, he went way further than them. This was partly down to the woman he married, a lady called Jezebel, who was the daughter of the Sidonian king. Jezebel worshiped the Canaanite fertility god Baal, and wasn't content for this worship to take place alongside worship of the God of the Jews. She wanted absolute devotion to her deity, and brooked no opposition. Ahab seems to have been weak-minded enough to simply give in to her. Jezebel saw it as her job to completely eradicate all worship of God, to seek out and kill the remaining prophets still loyal to him, and to encourage Ahab to also rise up against them, as well as to reign with utter terror, injustice, and immorality.

Naboth's vineyard is probably the moral low point of Ahab's reign. It is recorded in 1 Kings 21. Ahab wanted a vineyard belonging to a neighbour of his. However, when he asked if he could buy it, all his offers were refused. Like a spoiled child Ahab went home and sulked. Jezebel noticed and told him not to be so weak. She also told him she would deal with the matter at hand. As usual she took charge, and it meant the end of Naboth. Jezebel paid off the town official, who in turn paid off some men to lie before a town meeting that Naboth had cursed God. The punishment in those days for such blasphemy was stoning to death, and that is what happened to poor Naboth.

The pure wickedness and deceitfulness of this plan (not to mention the irony of Jezebel, herself a blasphemer and hater of God, encouraging someone to be put to death for allegedly doing the same), reminds me of the shameful duplicity of the chief priests of the Jews when Jesus was put on trial for blasphemy. First they brought forward witnesses who they had primed to lie about him, and then later on, when Jesus was on trial before the Roman governor Pontius Pilate, John 19:15 records them having the cheek to say, "We have no king but Caesar," when they in actual fact hated Roman rule and saw the worship of the Roman emperor (Caesar) as wicked blasphemy against the God they claimed to worship. They got Jesus crucified, and Ahab got his vineyard, but in each case there followed severe judgment. Jerusalem was destroyed forty years later by the same Romans the Jewish priests had tried to curry favor with, and Ahab had a very unpleasant encounter with the great prophet Elijah (who I will not mention in any more detail here, but about whom many excellent books have been written), who informed him about his upcoming death and the destruction of his whole dynasty. Ahab actually repented at this news, and God was gracious enough to spare him from the immediacy of his family's destruction. However, when confronted by another prophet Micaiah in 1 Kings 22, Ahab was less willing to listen, and his death was set. It seems his repentance was motivated by fear, and unfortunately didn't bring about a lasting change in him.

Ahab's death is well documented in the Bible. The story of it is told in both 1 Kings and, unusually for a king of the northern land, in 2 Chronicles (chapter 18). In these passages we get a fascinating glimpse into the spiritual realm and God's heavenly throne room. It appears here that God has had enough of Ahab's wickedness and decided it is time for his reign to come to an immediate end. The measure for carrying out this plan is to raise up false prophets to assure the king he will have victory in a battle that will instead bring about his demise. Sure enough there are plenty of people around who are willing to say exactly what Ahab wants to hear, and Ahab even now hasn't learned to obey the truth when it is inconvenient to him. He simply thinks the prophet Micaiah hates him, and is wishfully thinking Ahab will soon die. The prophet is summarily punished and Ahab, supported rather foolishly by Jehoshaphat, the otherwise good king of Judah, goes into battle and to his death. So ended the reign and the life of one of the most infamous of kings in all literature.

TO THINK ABOUT

Ahab put political security above faith in God. It was convenient for him to acquiesce to Jezebel's will because it kept his alliance with Sidon strong and enabled his land to have peace and prosperity, but at the expense of his and his nation's soul. What is your ultimate authority, your ultimate priority?

Is infamy worth it? Some people would prefer to be remembered for bad rather than live mundane anonymous lives. According to Susan Atkins, a serial killer and follower of the Charles Manson cult: "We wanted to do a crime that the world would have to stand up and take notice."[1] This is of course sick and immoral to say the least, and is based on either a lack of belief in any life after death or a twisted desire to somehow enjoy their desired version of hell. However, the Bible tells us: "And just as each person is destined to die once and after that comes judgment" (Hebrews 9:27). It also says that there is a place where those who reject God go. It is not a destination of any sort of enjoyment, but rather a place of punishment, regret, and suffering. We know little about hell except to be sure that it is a place which is both eternal and to be avoided at all costs. Jesus himself referred to a place "where there will be weeping and gnashing of teeth" (Matthew 25:30b). This suggests that in hell people will regret their past choices and re-live the horror of their wickedness, but without any of the pleasure they got for their cruelty while on earth.

What would we like as an epitaph of our life? I would hope that we would want to shun absolutely the sort of infamy with which Ahab, Jezebel (whose very name is a byword for evil!), and any number of psychopathic killers are associated. I would also hope that we would all want to aspire to something positive. For example, I would like to be thought of as someone who was faithful to God, and who made a positive difference to people's lives.

Will we be missed and mourned for, one day? There was a king in Judah called Jehoram, of whom it is said: "No one was sorry when he died" (2 Chronicles 21:20). How sad is that? Or perhaps we should ask, "How awful was he?" We cannot simply hope or wish for a nice epitaph, however. We can start today by

---

1. Psychopaths in Fact and Fiction, "In their own words . . .," Susan Atkins, line 4.

consciously thinking about and then acting on ensuring our epitaph, our legacy, is a good one, a godly one.

Ahab was a bit like the Pharisees who recognized the power of Jesus but chose to lie about him and to discredit him before the people. Therefore they were absolutely culpable for rejecting Christ. Ahab was also culpable because he saw God's power at work, most notably in the contest on Mount Carmel, when God, through the prophet Elijah, sent down fire from heaven (recorded in 1 Kings 18). He also recognized when prophets spoke the truth about events, most notably a scene in 1 Kings 22 when Micaiah prophesied about his upcoming death. However, he invariably refused to listen to what he knew to be the truth, and for that he is both judged and remembered (with notoriety). How do we respond to truth, no matter how inconvenient and unpalatable it might be? With a sort of self-righteous indignance or with humble acceptance and repentance? Our decision will ultimately go a long way to deciding how we are remembered.[2]

---

2. Some excerpts from a talk given by Paul Round at Hounslow Evangelical Church on the 8 February 2015 have been used in this chapter. My thanks to Paul for his permission to use the talk he gave for this purpose.

5

Jehu—Zeal without Grace

2 Kings 9–10

JEHU WAS A KING of the northern kingdom of Israel, and the means by which God brought judgment on the house of Ahab. He was a former army officer of King Ahab, whose accession to the throne was prophesied back in Ahab's time through the prophet Elijah. Jehu was anointed king at the order of God through Elisha, organized a bloody coup against the regime, and reigned for twenty-eight years. He was arguably the nearest a king of that northern kingdom got to actually following God. He cleaned up the awful legacy of Ahab and his family, he smashed down the altars of worship to the Canaanite idol Baal, and seemed to be God's man. Well he was certainly used by God to inflict judgment.[1]

Jezebel was still alive as the queen mother, and her influence was still felt in the kingdom as she had the ear of her sons Ahaziah and Joram who reigned after Ahab. However, Joram was swiftly put to death by Jehu, and in a somewhat grisly event Jehu ordered Jezebel's death. He turned up at the palace, and Jezebel decided

---

1. For most of us the thought of God inflicting judgment on people is somewhat uncomfortable and raises some difficult questions. For a great look at this and other difficult questions about God's character, Martin G. Kuhrt's *God is Good* is well worth a read.

to make herself up. It is not clear from the account in 2 Kings 9 if she was even in her old age trying to seduce him (it is very likely that Jezebel had been a very attractive woman who was well used to getting her way with men), or if she actually knew her fate was sealed and decided to leave this earth with her pride intact. Whatever her motivation, this was her last act. Her eunuchs, at Jehu's prompting, threw her from her window down on to the courtyard below.[2] Knowing her character, it is likely that she had been a cruel, demanding, and violent mistress, and I would have thought they were only too glad to be rid of her. Jezebel died in the fall and, as Elijah had prophesied some years earlier, horses trampled her body including the one Jehu was riding, so that by the time they bothered to bury her there wasn't much left.

Not stopping there, Jehu exacted revenge on the king of Judah, who was also called Ahaziah. He was in league with Ahab's family, and Jehu dispatched him too, along with every possibly member of Ahab's family that he could find. He was full of zeal for his commission as a purveyor of judgment. Indeed, so thoroughly did he carry out this plan that he went too far. In the prophetic book of Hosea, there is a condemnation of Jehu's brutality, and a warning that his own descendants would be wiped out in the same place where he had massacred Ahab's descendants – the Jezreel Valley (see Hosea 1:4–5).

In 2 Kings 10 Jehu kept up his cleansing of the land by luring the priests and worshipers of Baal to a feast, apparently in honor of that idol. However, Jehu's plan was to find out who was a Baal worshiper, get them all in one place, and then have them summarily executed. Jehu was clearly a cunning and clever man. Although

---

2. Eunuchs in the ancient world were men who had been castrated. They were impotent and didn't have a sex drive, because of the procedure that had been carried out on them. They often served in close proximity to the king and his family. They were seen as useful for two reasons: First, they wouldn't be distracted by thoughts of women or marriage, and so could give themselves completely to their master's/mistress's affairs. Second, as men in close proximity and with access to the queen, princesses, and the king's harem (the many women available to him), they would have been no threat to the women's reputation or competition to the king for their affections.

brutal, what he did made sense. His plan meant all the followers of Baal were removed, and those who did not worship Baal were spared.

However, Jehu (as well as being a sadistic killer!) failed to wholeheartedly serve and worship God. It seems Elisha knew what sort of man he was, as when he sent the prophets to anoint Jehu as king, he warned them with these words: "Say to him, 'This is what the LORD says: I anoint you to be the king over Israel.' Then open the door and run for your life!" (2 Kings 9:3b). Apparently, not many people got close to Jehu and lived! He was undoubtedly a very dangerous individual who brooked no opposition.

Jehu looked like God's man for Israel (as had Saul, the first of all Jewish kings, many generations earlier), but was a bloodthirsty disappointment. Although he did destroy the altars to Baal (even turning one of them into a public toilet—check it out in 2 Kings 10:27!) and killed the worshipers of that idol, he did not turn from the residual idolatry inherited from the first king of the ten tribes, Jeroboam. He reversed the worst excesses of Ahab and his sons, but failed to truly turn himself or Israel back to God. Like Jeroboam before him, Jehu was used by God as an agent of judgment, carried out his initial calling well, was promised a kingdom and a dynasty (Jehu was actually promised by God that it would survive for four generations [see 2 Kings 10:30]), but didn't seem to actually have a relationship with God or walk in his ways.

TO THINK ABOUT

Righteous anger or self-righteous revenge? Jehu and Jesus both showed righteous anger. The event of Jesus throwing tables around in the temple recorded in all the Gospels (for example John 2:13 21) is an example of justified anger. Jehu was also justified at first because he was fulfilling God's judgment on the house of Ahab. However, the problem with anger is, to paraphrase the Greek philosopher Aristotle, it is very difficult to be angry to the right degree, with the right person in the right way, and at the right time. Our anger can make us do foolish, sinful, and irrational things.

Jehu's righteous anger sadly turned into a self-righteous crusade against anyone and anything, and he was in the end condemned for it. He knew what was right but ended up being almost as bad a tyrant as Ahab, whose heritage he destroyed.

Jehu acted in justice (at least at first) but without mercy. Consider Micah 6:8, which says: "No, O people, the LORD has told you what is good, and this is what he requires of you: to do what is right, to love mercy, and to walk humbly with your God." Jehu obviously hadn't read the memo (in fairness Micah was written after his death), particularly with regard to loving mercy. It does suggest a lack of real relationship with God. Clearly God's anointing was on him, just as it was clearly on Saul and Jeroboam, but neither of them seemed to actually know God either. Jehu acted more like the Crusaders or the Jewish Zealots of Jesus' time, for example Barabbas, meting out justice supposedly on God's behalf, but not stopping to think if it was the right thing to do. Elisha lived in Jehu's time, but there is no word of any contact between the two of them after Elisha anointed Jehu to be king. It is doubtful Jehu would have listened to any reproach once he was king, and indeed it would have been incredibly dangerous (most likely fatal!) for anyone to do so.

Are we known more for what we are against than what we are for? We must be known first of all for being followers of Jesus. Many in society will characterize Christians as being opposed to certain things or even people. Sometimes this is blatantly unfair, but often they have a point. Although we should not be quiet in the face of social injustice or issues of ethics or morality, these should not define us. We are to preach Christ and his love for humanity which is open to all, and to endeavor to always keep this front and center of any activism we might undertake.

Romans 12:14–18 gives an alternative to Jehu's approach. We live under the new covenant, a covenant of grace which was ratified by Christ's death on the cross. We are to express this by showing grace to others, even our enemies. We are called to be forgiving, to love our enemies, and to leave any thoughts of revenge in God's hands. Jesus talks in very challenging language about this in the Sermon on the Mount (see Matthew 5:38–48).

Jehu was the leader of a nation which at times executed God's judgment on surrounding nations, and at others (such as his time) the judgment of God on those within the nation. His circumstances are very different from ours, yet even with that in mind Jehu is still condemned for his over zealousness and seeming love of violence, and certainly is not an example to follow.

6

Joash—A Great Start but a Bad End
2 Kings 11–12; 2 Chronicles 22:10—24:27

JOASH, SOMETIMES CALLED JEHOASH, was a king of Judah who was crowned at a very early age, and God's hand was certainly upon him. He survived an attempt by Queen Athaliah to wipe out the line of David. He was just two years old when Athaliah took the throne of Israel (the only woman to reign in either of the two kingdoms). She forcibly declared herself queen when she heard that Jehu had killed her son Ahaziah, but Joash was hidden away by his aunt and was spared from her rage. For six years she reigned, no doubt in the spirit of Jezebel her mother, a byword for wickedness and ungodliness. In all that time, Joash was kept hidden in the temple buildings. (This reminds me of the film *The Pianist* where a young Jewish man in Poland is saved from deportation to the death camps and then hidden in a room in the city for years undetected by the Nazis.) Then her enemies took their chance. No doubt very unpopular, even among the army and her own guards, she was brutally deposed, frog-marched out of the temple to be executed outside even while the seven-year-old king was being crowned.

Joash reigned under the advice and counsel of a great man of God, the priest Jehoiada, who was the husband of his erstwhile rescuer. He did very well, breaking the influence of idol worship and arranging for the restoration of the temple which had been used for the worship of false gods. He was even responsible enough to notice when the Levites were being frivolous, perhaps even dishonest, with the money and other resources. He asked Jehoiada to sort this out, and the bad practices were stopped. The good example from the palace filtered through and the workmen and contractors were honest in their labors, as well as fair. The Levites were still given what was rightfully theirs.

However, it then went horribly wrong. The turning point was the death of Jehoiada. Once he had departed, it was as though Joash lived and reigned like a ship without a rudder. Bad advisers got his ear and were able to influence him, a little bit like his distant predecessor Rehoboam, but this time with even more spectacularly bad results. Joash turned against worship of God and was persuaded to reverse his reforms, going back to permitting and even endorsing idol worship. This brought him a rebuke from Jehoiada's son Zechariah. Stung by the criticism, and feeling himself to be beyond reproach, Joash acted with rage, not even granting him the courtesy of being executed outside the temple as Athaliah had been. Zechariah was executed right there before the altar itself. Joash may have been a descendant of David, but his response to godly, prophetic criticism couldn't have been more different. With his final breath Zechariah cursed those who were executing him, and Joash's fate was sealed. Not only was he in serious trouble, but so was his kingdom.

At this point the narratives in 2 Kings and 2 Chronicles differ, but what is consistent between them is that God's curse was on Judah and he now aided the Aramean army in bringing judgment on the country. Many were killed, and Joash (according to the account in 2 Chronicles) was injured. The account in 2 Kings mentions that he turned over the temple treasuries to their army in a final act of betrayal of God and his former mentor in an effort to spare his life and keep his throne. This worked in the short term, but Joash had made too many enemies, and was soon assassinated, apparently by some of his previous advisers who wished to vindicate Zechariah. For me, Joash is probably the most tragic of the kings of Judah. It all started so well, but his end was so ignominious that he wasn't even buried in the royal cemetery.

TO THINK ABOUT

Let's look at the danger of complacency in our faith. Complacency is a very easy trap to fall or slide into. Joash may have believed that his good works in his early years were sufficient to "keep in God's good books" indefinitely, or perhaps he decided he simply didn't need God anymore. Like Jeroboam and countless others, power sadly corrupted him. As for us, we must always be on the lookout for signs of apathy and complacency in our own lives, be it toward our closest relationships (especially, if applicable, our marriages) or our faith in God. If we are not continually looking to move on in our faith then the reality is we are probably going backwards. I see it like walking against one of those moving walkways you find in airport terminals. If you walk against it you make progress, but if you stop walking you will find yourself a long way back before you know it.

We need our own personal faith and commitment, not relying on the faith of others, for example parents. There is an old saying that God has no grandchildren in heaven. Each person is called to account for their own faith and their own life; we cannot rely on anyone else. When I was in my early days as a Christian, as a teenager, I remember the vicar of the church warning us that he wouldn't be standing with us holding our hands when we go before God as he would be too busy giving account for his own life. We have to take responsibility for ourselves and be able to walk with Christ not simply because someone else tells us to or keeps us moving in the right direction. Once Joash lost the directing influence of Jehoiada he soon departed from the path of righteousness suggesting he had been living out someone else's faith the whole time rather than his own.

Joash seems to have been easily led, first for good, and understandably given he was a child at the time. However, after Jehoiada's death Joash, though by now a grown man, seems to have all too easily been led astray by bad advisers (remember Rehoboam!) who convinced him to live for himself rather than God. We must take a balanced line here. It is vital we are ready to listen to advice, and to thoughtfully and prayerfully consider it, but we must also be ready and confident to make our own decisions and to stand against the advice of, and even the people giving it themselves, when it will harm us and cause us to act wrongly.

Pride seemed to prevent Joash from turning back to God. Pride is an exceedingly dangerous thing. It convinces us we are right and will not allow us to consider any challenge to our way of life or thinking. When we are proud, God cannot work in our lives. Let's make it our commitment to avoid pride at all costs.

7

Jehoash and Jeroboam II—
Powerful Kings but a Godless Land

2 Kings 13:10–25; 14:23–29; 2 Chronicles 25

THESE TWO MEN ARE not the most well-known of kings, and indeed they take up very little space in the Bible. However, on a military and economic level they were very notable and very successful (as was the similarly overlooked King Omri, Ahab's father). Jehoash actually took Jerusalem and effectively ruled both Israelite kingdoms, reversing the fortunes of what had been a declining and vulnerable state that he inherited. His son and successor Jeroboam II continued the revival of fortunes, holding the territory his father had taken and expanding the kingdom, even taking the notable prize of Damascus from Syria. The reason they are worth having a chapter on here is the contrast between worldly success and spiritual fruit and legacy.

Jehoash (sometimes confusingly referred to as Joash) was the grandson of Jehu, and became king while Joash was still on the throne of Judah. His reign lasted a relatively short sixteen years, and when it began it looked as though the kingdom would soon be overrun. Apparently, in his father Jehoahaz's time, the army had been virtually decimated by the Syrians (see 2 Kings 13:7). After a short summary of Jehoash's reign, which is primarily concerned with his relationship with God (he was condemned as godless), some notable events are shared.

First, at the beginning of Jehoash's reign Elisha was still alive, but very ill. Jehoash had the sense to realize Elisha would be a big loss to the nation. So he went to visit him with great mourning and tears. Elisha gave him a challenge to show his faith in God. Jehoash was willing to do what the prophet said but apparently wasn't enthusiastic enough. I think, reading between the lines, he didn't show enough faith. The upshot of this last encounter between Elisha and a king of Israel was that Israel would defeat their enemy the Arameans (equivalent of Syria today), but it wouldn't be as comprehensive or long-lasting a victory as it would have been had Jehoash showed more faith when tested by Elisha.

Soon after that, Amaziah king of Judah was enabled by God to win a big victory over the Edomites (descendants of Jacob's twin brother Esau). Buoyed by this victory, Amaziah decided it would be an opportune time to attack Israel too, as there had been some previous trouble between the nations. However, Amaziah turned out to be a big disappointment spiritually speaking, as despite doing God's will early in his reign, and despite being promised by a prophet military success if he trusted God, he decided to take the idols of the Edomites and worship them. Such stupidity, not to mention wickedness, in the face of God's help, was never going to end well, and Amaziah's army was roundly defeated by Jehoash's army. Jehoash didn't stop with the defeat of the army of Judah, but promptly marched on Jerusalem plundering gold and silver from the temple and taking Amaziah prisoner. It seems Amaziah was allowed to return to Jerusalem, but as a vassal king who had to pay tribute and pledge loyalty to his overseer Jehoash and his successor (Jeroboam II).

That story suggests that Jehoash did well more because of the foolishness and wickedness of his rival Amaziah than from his own goodness or wisdom. He profited from another's stupidity and from the removal of God's blessing from them.

Jeroboam II likewise benefited, extending the kingdom even further during his reign. He was used by God to relieve the suffering in the land (see 2 Kings 14:26–27) and perhaps wasn't a very unpleasant ruler, but unfortunately he too refused to acknowledge God or do his will. It looked like the nation might prosper for a long period, and perhaps even completely swallow up Judah, however some very dark clouds were on the horizon.

Amos, a prophet who lived in Judah but prophesied mainly about the northern kingdom, operated in Jeroboam II's time. He warned the people against complacency, and made it clear that things were not as they should be. Not only had the king and his people turned from God, but they were also presiding over and living in an inherently unjust society. Here is a small flavor of Amos's message: "'My people have forgotten how to do right,' says the LORD. 'Their fortresses are filled with wealth taken by theft and violence'" (Amos 3:10). He also told them in no uncertain times that judgment was coming, even promising that "I will bring the dynasty of King Jeroboam to a sudden end" (Amos 7:9b).

Jeroboam II's idolatry and refusal to acknowledge God ultimately sealed the fate of Israel, which fell very far and very fast after his death. God had promised Jehu that his descendants would reign in Israel to the fourth generation (see 2 Kings 10:30). At Jeroboam's death that was now complete. His son was deposed and assassinated, and Jehu's dynasty was finished. We can only suppose that had one of Jehu's descendants honored God then things may have turned out differently. However, the end of Jehu's dynasty meant the writing was on the wall for the whole northern kingdom. The land would soon fall under the control of the superpower of the time, Assyria, who were infamous for their violence and cruelty. Approximately thirty years after the death of Jeroboam II, the final king Hoshea rebelled, was captured and imprisoned, and the people exiled from the land to Assyria itself. And so, in 722 BC, the northern kingdom fell and was no more.

TO THINK ABOUT

Worldly success doesn't necessarily correlate with godliness or God's approval. Many are storing up treasures on this earth but will find that this short-term gain was not worth the eternal cost of ignoring God. Jesus says in Matthew 16:25–26: "If you try to hang on to your life, you will lose it. But if you give up your life for my sake, you will save it. And what do you benefit if you gain the whole world but lose your own soul? Is anything worth more than your soul?" Again Jesus says: "Don't store up treasures here on earth, where moths eat them and rust destroys them, and where thieves break in and steal. Store your treasures in heaven, where moths and rust cannot destroy, and thieves do not break in and steal" (Matthew 6:19–20). Finally, in a passage aimed at believers, Jesus says that even if we have a faith in God, and have experienced his salvation, we can still miss out on God's eternal rewards (even though we will still enter heaven itself) if our attitude to God and our life is wrong. "Watch out! Don't do your good deeds publicly, to be admired by others, for you will lose the reward from your Father in heaven" (Matthew 6:1).

Worldly success for those who turn their backs on God is short term. Once things start to go wrong, the downward spiral can be very rapid indeed. If things are going wrong for you, it is not necessarily God's judgment, but it is always worth checking your heart, your actions, your relationships, and being open to humbling yourself before God. We also never know how long we have left on this earth. In Matthew 6:27, Jesus asks this pertinent question: "Can all your worries add a single moment to your life?" He also gives a striking message in the parable of the rich fool who got very rich, only cared about himself, and thought nothing of God, which is recorded thus: "But God said to him, 'You fool! You will die this very night. Then who will get everything you worked for?'" (Luke 12:20).

The successes of Jehoash and Jeroboam II were more down to God's judgment on Judah than any sense they deserved it. In a similar way, Assyria was able to destroy the northern kingdom as God's instrument of judgment against it. But this didn't mean that there was no case for them to answer before God. Their day of reckoning would come, and it did. The prophet Nahum talks about that day in graphic terms in the Old Testament book of the same name. Sometimes we may be messing up badly in our spiritual lives and in our relationships yet things seem to be going well for us. Don't be fooled. There will be a time to give an account, and we need to be ready, and also willing to make peace with God and turn back to him as soon as we realize we are not right before him. As we've explored before, complacency can be very dangerous!

8

Hezekiah—A King Given Extra Time

2 Kings 18–20; 2 Chronicles 29–32

HEZEKIAH REIGNED FOR TWENTY-NINE years, a good amount of time albeit shorter than a number of other kings. Yet the account of his kingship is given the most total coverage in the Bible of all the kings of the divided kingdoms. He is widely seen as one of the best and most godly of the kings of Israel. He had to undo a lot of the damage done by his father Ahaz who, despite reigning a comparatively short sixteen years, had undone a lot of the good work of his father Jotham and grandfather Uzziah (sometimes referred to as Azariah). Hezekiah desired to see God's name glorified and the worship of idols purged. He re-opened the temple which had been brazenly closed by Ahaz. He closed all other sites of worship to idols, going further than Uzziah and Jotham had in dealing with these bad practices.

Uzziah was a king of much acclaim, but he became arrogant and proud in his later years, eventually being struck down with leprosy as a judgment on him. The great prophet Isaiah wrote wistfully about his death in Isaiah 6, when he had his great vision of heaven, suggesting Uzziah was a much-loved king. Isaiah continued his ministry through the reigns of Jotham and Ahaz, but was most associated with Hezekiah. One of Hezekiah's purges was to destroy an ancient relic of Israel. The "Nehushtan" was a bronze snake that God had commanded Moses to make so that people would look at it and be healed of the snake bites they had been afflicted with as a result of disobeying God in the wilderness (an event which took place in Numbers 21:4–9). Unfortunately (and, I would add, inevitably), the people of Israel by the time of Hezekiah had decided to worship this metal object, which was idolatry in God's sight, and so it had to go. It took Hezekiah to finally remove it (2 Kings 18:4).

Hezekiah was able to win miraculous battles against superior enemy forces due to his trust in God and humbling of himself and the people before him. He also restored temple worship to a priority and a focus not seen for many years. The celebration of Passover which he ordered was a major sign of revival and a return to worship of the true and living God. He even bridged the divide between the two parts of Israel, reaching out to the people in the former kingdom of the north who had escaped the Assyrian imposed exile, bringing some of them to this great Passover celebration. Hezekiah was closer to success in uniting the divided nations of the Jews by spiritual means than anyone had managed using military means.

Hezekiah, at one point in his life, became ill and was told by the great prophet Isaiah, no less, that he would soon die. We don't know if this was due to some sin he had committed, but we do know that he humbled himself before God and was granted fifteen extra years. Hezekiah's extra life span is unparalleled in scripture. The Lord even proved this miracle by making the shadow of the sun retreat in reversal of its normal pattern, a miracle only possible for the creator himself (see 2 Kings 20:1–11 for the account of this incredible story).

Unfortunately it seems that Hezekiah didn't necessarily use this time for the best. Like many a king or other ruler before and since, he became proud. Presumably to impress the powerful Babylonians and to show off his wealth, he foolishly decided to show a delegation of them the temple and palace precincts and everything in them. Isaiah the prophet turned up again, this time to prophesy that Hezekiah's friendship with Babylon would explode in his face as that would be the country which would be used to take control of Judah and exile its people in a future time. His final recorded thoughts were a response to this, and sadly showed a selfish side to his character. Hezekiah breathed a sigh of relief and thought to himself: "At least it won't happen on my watch!" A sad and disappointing footnote in the life of a king who did such amazing things to serve God.

TO THINK ABOUT

Hezekiah did not have a good start in life in a spiritual sense. His father Ahaz was an ungodly king who encouraged the worship of false idols and who degraded the temple. He may have been aware of his grandfather Jotham in his early years, and perhaps had even taken a good example from him, but I think for many of us Hezekiah is a great encouragement that God can use us in spite of our parents. Hezekiah's upbringing did not define him. He was able to choose his own way and chose for God. Many come to know God even though their parents are either ambivalent or even opposed to the things of God. There is a certain strength and character in a person who has personally chosen to live for the Lord and commit themselves to him. We must never rule people out, as far as the kingdom of God is concerned, even when they have no godly heritage at all. God still searches for them and calls them to himself. He still has a claim on their life. Maybe you are in that situation yourself. You have chosen to follow Jesus (or maybe you are thinking about taking that step) but none of your family is with you. Be encouraged that you are not alone. The Lord is with you and many go before you who have stood firm in Christ even when everyone has opposed them.

If, on the other hand, you are a parent who longs for your children to accept Jesus, there are two pieces of news; one good and one bad.

The bad news is that you cannot guarantee or force your children to be followers of Jesus. They must make that choice for themselves, and it is ultimately between them and God.

The good news is that your prayers, your example, your teaching of your children, gives them a better chance of accepting Jesus. Although they do have to decide for themselves, loving and godly parents are more likely to beget children who choose Christ. So, persevere in your prayers for your children, even when they seem to turn away, and keep loving them and showing them God's love for them even when it is not reciprocated. Hezekiah, I imagine, saw that his son Manasseh was turning into a pretty unpleasant man who had turned his back on God. He never saw the full extent of the grim and cruel nature of Manasseh's reign, but he also never saw Manasseh's eventual repentance and turning back to the God his father worshiped.

The danger of religious objects and traditions is that, although usually holding an important significance, they can easily take on an importance in people's lives that is unhealthy. They can be relied on almost as substitutes for real faith in Christ, or even an insurance policy which those using them believe somehow makes them right with God. In the worst excesses of ritualism or religious relics, an object can be worshiped. This had happened with the bronze snake. Something that reminded the Jews of God's mercy had been corrupted into becoming a snare which turned the people's attention away from God. We need to be careful in our own lives to avoid idolatry, and in our worship to avoid clinging too tightly to traditions or religious artifacts (for example pictures, crucifixes, or even church buildings).

If you have been unusually blessed by God, for example seeing a vision of him or experiencing a great work of healing or deliverance, praise him, but don't allow this to make you arrogant or self-righteous. The apostle Paul was similarly blessed in an unusual way, but was glad that God kept him humble even though it involved difficulty, through a phenomenon Paul referred to as having a thorn in the flesh (see 2 Corinthians 12:1–10).[1]

1. R.T. Kendall's book on the subject, *The Thorn in the Flesh*, is also well worth a read.

Contrast Paul with King Henry VIII, who was the founder of the Church of England. He was absolutely certain he was God's man and brooked no dissent, challenge, or opposition. Consequently, he was one of the worst tyrants to sit on the throne of England, and presided over a reign of terror in which thousands were executed at his whim. Here was an example of a man who believed he was above the law, the church, and any other authority. Once someone's heart is hardened they are on a very destructive path (consider the Pharaoh of Egypt who stood in the way of the Israelites, even when the plagues were raining down on his people—see Exodus 5–14), and we ourselves in our humble lives must be careful not to become too proud of our achievements or too embittered by our losses, but ask our Lord to help us stay on an even keel in those times.

9

Manasseh—God's Boundless Grace

2 Kings 21:1–18; 2 Chronicles 33:1–20

WE SHOULD NOT BE too harsh on Hezekiah really, because the kings on either side of him, his father Ahaz and son Manasseh, were the worst two kings to sit on the throne of Judah (Queen Athaliah also deserving a dishonorable mention!). Hezekiah's reign sticks out as a beacon of light in comparison to theirs, even if he was found wanting at times.

Manasseh actually made Ahaz look tame with his blatant idolatry, horrendous pagan practices, and cruel tyranny. He also reigned for the longest time of any king of Israel or Judah, a whopping fifty-five years (ten of which were probably served as co-regent with his father Hezekiah), so there was much to endure.

Time and again prophets were sent to Manasseh, and time and again he ignored them (I am guessing some of them lost their lives in the process). Tradition has it that Isaiah the prophet who had been so influential was executed under Manasseh's order, apparently by being sawn in two! (The New Testament book of Hebrews makes mention of this awful punishment in its account of the suffering of the men and women of faith in the Old Testament—see Hebrews 11:37.)

It wasn't just the prophets who suffered. Chillingly, the Bible records: "Manasseh also murdered many innocent people until Jerusalem was filled from one end to the other with innocent blood" (2 Kings 21:16a).

Manasseh's cruelty extended to his pagan practices. They involved child sacrifice even of his own children, which took place in the valley of Ben-Hinnom. This valley, which is to the south of the old city of Jerusalem, was known by the time of Jesus around 700 years later as Gehenna. Translated into English that means garbage tip, and that name to the Jews of Jesus' time was also synonymous with hell and judgment. Manasseh's wicked practices (as well as those of his grandfather Ahaz, who did similar) gave that place a name to be shuddered at. In modern times, there are similar places where great evil has taken place, and people who visit them often tell of the very feeling they get when they are there. The concentration and death camps from the Second World War are just such places of horror and shuddering. The same can be said (albeit on a smaller scale of death toll) of the houses and names of serial killers. For example, if you were in the UK in the early 1990s you only have to hear the names Fred and Rosemary West, or even the street in Gloucester they lived in—Cromwell Street—to wince with the memory of the news reports detailing their depraved wickedness and the horror of their house.

Manasseh not only behaved in a more depraved manner than even the Amorites who were removed from the same land because of their wickedness, but he literally shook his fist at God. He returned to the worship of the stars and the moon (which it is believed was the prevalent religion of the city the first Israelite patriarch Abraham came from), and even set up an idol right in the most holy place of the temple. It seemed that everything Manasseh did was aimed at stirring up God's wrath.

And sure enough, judgment came. Eventually Israel's Assyrian overlords turned up in Jerusalem (no doubt Manasseh had unwisely rebelled against their rule in his own strength), and Manasseh was carted off like a farm animal with a ring through his nose to Babylon (which at that time was still part of the Assyrian empire). There he was held captive and in chains, and it was there that we see one of the most incredible about turns in the whole of the Bible. I will leave it in the chronicler's own words: "But while in deep distress, Manasseh sought the LORD his God and sincerely humbled himself before the God of his ancestors" (2 Chronicles 33:12). Amazingly the very next verse tells us that God heard his prayer, answered it, and enabled Manasseh to return to Jerusalem where he attempted to undo some of the damage he had done.

The repentance of Manasseh is indicative of the prophetic word to Solomon regarding turning from one's wicked ways, a statement often used as a call to prayer and repentance in times of national difficulty: "Then if my people who are called by my name will humble themselves and pray and seek my face and turn from their wicked ways, I will hear from heaven and will forgive their sins and restore their land" (2 Chronicles 7:14).

TO THINK ABOUT

It must have been near impossible to live out your faith when Manasseh was king. Many Christians today live under persecution, whether it be from family, society, an autocratic ruler, or religious intolerance. In many areas of the world, just to admit to being a Christian will cost you your life, or at least life in a labor camp. Some examples of this include North Korea and Somalia. Other nations might be less extreme, but yet will still discriminate against Christians and, especially in Islamic states, crack down very hard on Muslim-background believers in Christ. Even in democratic countries where freedom of religion is sacrosanct, there can be pressure to conform or penalties for sharing your faith or having certain views that aren't in keeping with the prevailing moral code.

In the New Testament, both Jesus and the disciples who wrote the letters assume that being persecuted for one's faith is to be expected and indeed is the default position for Christians. That is not very comforting, but here is one thing Jesus said: "If any of you wants to be my follower, you must give up on your own way, take up your cross, and follow me" (Matthew 16:24b). To live for

God means giving him our all, not just when it is convenient or popular, but in all circumstances. After all, Jesus literally took up his cross to make us right with God, and to guarantee life with him in this world and in the next.

How do we respond to God's judgment? Manasseh was horrendous in his kingship, but he did have the wisdom and the humility to repent before God when he was punished. After that he changed his ways and began to undo some of the damage he had carried out earlier in his reign. As I write this, we are still in the middle of the coronavirus pandemic which has gripped the world through most of 2020 and is still prevalent as we enter 2021. Clearly if God is all powerful then he could have stopped this virus if he so wished. The fact it still rages despite millions of people's prayers for it to be vanquished suggests that God wants to speak to us through these difficult times. The vaccine has been found and is beginning to be administered as I write, but there are still months of disruption ahead and the economic and mental health fallout will rumble on for years. So just what does God want to teach the world? Perhaps he desires that people will see their need for him, will realize just how frail humanity is, and will repent and pray to God for deliverance. When things go wrong in our lives it is always good to evaluate what we are doing and consider where we can change and what we can learn from our experiences. What I am not saying here is that all suffering is self-inflicted or somehow deserved. In the Bible Job suffered terribly through no fault of his own, for example. However, we tend to learn from hard times, and there are episodes of our lives where we have brought trouble on ourselves if we are honest (I know I have!). Our response in those times can be to thrash around looking for someone to blame and getting angry and bitter toward God or to throw ourselves at his feet, asking for his mercy and grace. For all his faults Manasseh was willing to do this. I am sure he went through all sorts of mental anguish before he got to that point, and it would have been hard for him to get over the memory and regret for his past sin and cruelty, but the bottom line is that he turned to God, and the Lord graciously heard his prayer.

This brings me to my final point in this chapter, and the one which the chapter is named for, and that is God's unbelievable grace toward repentant sinners. You might read this feeling that God couldn't possibly forgive you, that you are undeserving of his attention in any way. Well, the good news is firstly that you are not alone. We are all sinners who are utterly helpless when it comes to justifying ourselves before God. None of us can stand before him and expect his favor. The apostle Paul said: "for all have sinned and fall short of the glory of God" (Romans 3:23, ESV). Everyone is a wrongdoer at the end of the day, and we can only be saved by God's gift of grace. It was the death of God's one and only Son, given as a sacrifice to take our place, to take our punishment, which means that we can be set free from our rebellion against God, to be declared not guilty because he took our sins on himself, and to know his peace and favor now and forever. We each are recipients of this grace if we turn from our sins and hand our lives over to God. The apostle Paul knew this well. He had previously been a religious zealot who hated the name of Jesus Christ and who sought to eradicate all worship of him and to punish (even kill) the early Christians who believed in him. Like Manasseh, Paul turned from his God-opposing path to instead serving God, and so can you.

10

Josiah—Wholehearted Commitment

2 Kings 22:1—23:30; 2 Chronicles 34:1—35:27

AT LAST WE COME to Josiah, a king about who it is said there was never a king before or after him who served God so wholeheartedly. The same was said of Hezekiah but, as we have seen, he somewhat blotted his copybook in his later years. Josiah was something else. For loyalty and obedience to God he even surpassed the great king David. He cleansed the land of idolatry, and seems to have had jurisdiction over what had previously been the northern kingdom. Even more than Hezekiah, we see an effective unity of the two lands (and especially those faithful to the living God) in Josiah's reign. He was even the fulfillment of a prophecy made hundreds of years previously against Jeroboam and the place of idol worship he set up in Bethel: "At the LORD's command, a man of God from Judah went to Bethel, arriving there just as Jeroboam was approaching the altar to burn incense. Then at the LORD's command, he shouted, 'O altar, altar! This is what the LORD says: A child named Josiah will be born into the dynasty of David. On you he will sacrifice the priests from the pagan shrines who come here to burn incense, and human bones will be burned on you'" (1 Kings 13:1–2).

Josiah more than anyone fulfilled the hope of a future godly king. We read in Deuteronomy 17:18–20:

> When he sits on the throne as king, he must copy for himself this body of instruction on a scroll in the presence of the Levitical priests. He must always keep that copy with him and read it daily as long as he lives. That way he will learn to fear the Lord his God by obeying all the terms of these instructions and decrees. This regular reading will prevent him from becoming proud and acting as if he is above his fellow citizens. It will also prevent him from turning away from these commands in the smallest way. And it will ensure that he and his descendants will reign for many generations in Israel.

Josiah took the throne when he was eight years of age. The Bible tells us that eight years later, when sixteen years of age, he had some sort of conversion experience. The example of his father Amon was not a good one, but Josiah seems to have found God in spite of this. Four years later he started to remove the idol worship which was endemic in the land. After six further years he looked to begin the repair of the temple and the re-opening of it for the worship of God. Money was collected for this purpose from all over the land, including from the territories and remnants of the tribes of the old northern kingdom.

It is this renovation that sparks a significant moment in Josiah's reign. While cleaning up the temple, one of the priests found a scroll which had evidently been discarded during the previous misuse of the temple probably during Manasseh's reign. This scroll was read to Josiah, and he and his officials realized it was a portion of the Torah (the Jewish books of the law). Most historians today believe it was a part of or even the whole of the book of Deuteronomy. When Josiah heard these words, he realized just how far the nation had fallen from what God expected of them, and also just how much trouble they were in. For example, Deuteronomy 27 and 28 give an account of the curses and trouble which will come on the land and its people if Israel turns away from God. Josiah's response was that of someone in mourning.

First he tore his clothes (see 2 Chronicles 34:19). He then asked for help from someone who might be able to enquire of God on his and his people's behalf. The person who was found was a prophetess named Huldah. She confirmed that Israel was under severe judgment for its sin and its unfaithfulness to the God who had saved them from slavery in Egypt and who had gifted them the land they were now in. There was no other alternative but exile for the people (as decreed in Deuteronomy 28), however, Josiah's repentance and his willingness to serve God meant this judgment would be postponed by a generation. This was a similar message to that given to Hezekiah near the end of his life, but Josiah's response is much better. Instead of sitting back relieved that he wouldn't be exiled himself or live to see the land ravaged by invaders, Josiah ramped up his religious reforms. He stepped up his purges of all worship and all sacred places for other gods. He also continued with the repair of the temple and with ensuring that the Passover would be celebrated with great enthusiasm and pomp, even outdoing the celebrations which took place during Hezekiah's reign. He also took it upon himself to read the scroll to the people so they would hear the message for themselves. He ordered a solemn commitment to be made by the people to keep to the commands and expectations written within it.

During Josiah's reign the example of the king was wholeheartedly one of commitment to God, to his laws, and to ensuring the worship of God was the only acceptable practice in the land.

However, trouble was brewing. Assyria was weakening and Babylon was rising up as the new superpower. To the southwest, Egypt was also gaining in influence. Neco, the Egyptian Pharaoh, wanted to march through Judah on his way to assisting the Assyrians against the Babylonians. Josiah, no doubt wanting to be free of the Assyrian yoke which had long since plagued his land, did not want the Egyptians coming through to help them. He also was no doubt wary of allowing an enemy army on his territory. Therefore he decided to stop the Egyptian army in its tracks by marching out to fight it. The response of Pharaoh Neco was surprising. He said: "What do you want with me, king of Judah? I have no quarrel with you today! I am on my way to fight another nation, and God has told me to hurry! Do not interfere with God, who is with me, or he will destroy you" 2 Chronicles 35:21b). On hearing this, Josiah should really have hesitated. Huldah was no doubt still available for him to enquire of God, and the great prophet Jeremiah was also active at this time. However, Josiah seems not to have listened to Neco, nor to have enquired of God, because he marched out to fight anyway and was killed in battle. The people mourned for this great king, with Jeremiah acting as lamenter in chief. With Josiah's passing went the last realistic hope for Judah.

TO THINK ABOUT

We thought about epitaphs and legacies in the chapter on Ahab, in a negative sense. Here it is helpful to think about legacy in a positive sense, as we consider Josiah's good reign. Josiah is recorded as arguably the most godly king of Israel, one who stood alone in his commitment to God and to being a good example to the people in his worship of the Lord. It is a great legacy to have. We must not be content with the mundane, or be happy that generally we were nice people who never did anybody any harm. We should look to be cementing a legacy which is compelling to those who knew us and those who will go after us.

The apostle Paul challenged his readers to build with precious stones and valuable materials. What he meant was to question if they were acting and living out their faith, or if their faith was merely a shallow and half-hearted afterthought. We read in 1 Corinthians 3:11–15:

> For no one can lay any foundation other than the one we already have—Jesus Christ. Anyone who builds on that foundation may use a variety of materials—gold, silver, jewels, wood, hay, or straw. But on the judgment day, fire will reveal what kind of work each builder has done. The fire will show if a person's work has any value. If the work

survives, that builder will receive a reward. But if the
work is burned up, the builder will suffer great loss. The
builder will be saved, but like someone barely escaping
through a wall of flames.

Josiah's commitment to the word of God is an example to us all.
He must have had a very limited understanding of who God was
or how to worship him, yet even from a young age his heart was
inclined toward the Lord. When he came into contact with part
of the Bible, this commitment to serving the Lord went up con-
siderably. Josiah, even though he was king and had a lot of power,
humbly and willingly put himself under God's authority and set
about doing all he could to live in his service and to encourage the
people to do the same.

By contrast, all of us today have such easy access to the Bible.
It is readily available in shops, through internet companies, on
apps for mobile phones, and on the internet. We also have the
bonus of it being in a number of different translations, according
on our taste and also our reading ability. It is easy to take this for
granted and leave our Bibles to gather dust (or the web page or app
never being opened). However, the Bible is dynamite in our hands.
"In May 1928, the [British] Prime Minister Stanley Baldwin said,
'The Bible is a high explosive. But it works in strange ways and no
living man can tell or know how that book, in its journey through
the world, has startled the individual soul in ten thousand different
places into a new life, a new world, a new belief, a new conception,
a new faith.'"[1] It has been given by God to us to teach us about the
world, ourselves, and about God himself. It can change and trans-
form us if we will come under its authority and allow God to speak
through it by his Holy Spirit. "For the word of God is alive and
powerful. It is sharper than the sharpest two-edged sword, cutting
between soul and spirit, between joint and marrow. It exposes our
innermost thoughts and desires" (Hebrews 4:12). Many Christians
in persecuted nations have little or no access to the Bible, and
just owning one can be very dangerous. May we have the heart of

1. Gumbel, *Questions of Life*, 69

Josiah, who was transformed as a result of his encounter with these words of life.

Josiah was inspired by an encounter with God, and through reading God's word. However, his downfall was caused by his being unwilling to accept God's capacity to speak through unusual sources, in this case Pharaoh Neco. God uses all sorts of mediums to get our attention. The world itself is a testimony to God the creator and his Lordship over us. "They know the truth about God because he has made it obvious to them. For ever since the world was created, people have seen the earth and sky. Through everything God made, they can clearly see his invisible qualities—his eternal power and divine nature. So they have no excuse for not knowing God" (Romans 1:19–20).

11

Zedekiah—Time Is Running Out
2 Kings 24:18—25:7; 2 Chronicles 36:11-21

ZEDEKIAH WAS THE LAST in the line of a number of kings whose reigns were relatively short and who failed to live up to the promise of the laudable Josiah. In fact he was the last king to sit on the throne in Jerusalem. He inherited a realm which was completely dependent on, and answerable to, the superpower of that day, Babylon. He was only king because his nephew Jehoiachin (or Jeconiah as he was otherwise known) had been deposed and exiled to Babylon, and the king of Babylon decided that uncle Mattaniah would be a compliant "puppet" ruler, reigning under the name we know him as, Zedekiah.

From the warnings given in earlier scriptures it seems that the kingdom was still intact in Zedekiah's time only because Josiah had done what was right in God's sight and had postponed God's judgment on Judah. Each king who was allowed to reign had the opportunity to do what was right and God would enable them to be delivered from the dangers of invasion and destruction. I am not sure Zedekiah had this luxury, as it seems things were too far gone. It is certain that he inherited a much-diminished kingdom, not least in terms of the people in it. The brightest and best had been taken off in exile to Babylon in 605 BC, during Jehoiakim's reign. (These included a man called Daniel, whose exploits and life of faith are recorded in a very well worth reading book of the same name, also found in the Bible.)

The prophet Jeremiah advised Zedekiah to acquiesce to the Babylonians' demands and not to rebel against them because their fate was already sealed. However, Zedekiah did not listen. This is what 2 Chronicles says about him and his nation: "Zedekiah was a hard and stubborn man, refusing to turn to the LORD, the God of Israel . . . The LORD, the God of their ancestors, repeatedly sent his prophets to warn them, for he has compassion on his people and his Temple. But the people mocked these messengers of God and despised their words. They scoffed at the prophets until the LORD's anger could no longer be restrained and nothing could be done" (2 Chronicles 36:13b, 15–16). However, Zedekiah, though seeming to have no time for God, still somehow expected God to reward him and fight on his side.

Sadly Zedekiah caused much suffering to his people. Nebuchadnezzar king of Babylon, incensed by Zedekiah's rebellion, laid siege to Jerusalem and a great famine resulted which was so severe that people resorted to eating human excrement and even cannibalism. In 586 BC the city fell, the temple was destroyed and most of the rest of the people were exiled to Babylon. As for Zedekiah he suffered in the most horrendous terms. This is the account of his attempted escape and what followed: "But the Babylonian troops chased the king and overtook him on the plains of Jericho, for his men had all deserted him and scattered. They captured the king and took him to the king of Babylon at Riblah, where they pronounced judgment upon Zedekiah. They made Zedekiah watch as they slaughtered his sons. Then they gouged out Zedekiah's eyes, bound him in bronze chains, and led him away to Babylon" (2 Kings 25:5–7).

In a rather awful symmetry, the last king of Judah was captured by the very city (Jericho) where the Jews began their conquest of the promised land. Israel and Judah had been defeated and there seemed to be no hope. Some people escaped to Egypt, but that was a dead end. The hope would come from those in exile in Babylon, and help would come from an unexpected source. Jeremiah prophesied in chapter 25 of his book of prophecies that the exile would only last seventy years, and that the people, or at least a remnant, would be able to return to the land. In the last chapter of 2 Chronicles their return is summarized. Eventually the Babylonians were judged for their excesses and their mistreatment of the Jews, and their kingdom was overthrown by the Persians and Medes. The Persian king Cyrus was stirred up by God (although it is unclear if he was a worshiper of him) to allow the Jews home and to re-build a temple to him there (see 2 Chronicles 36:22–23).

So even in the midst of judgment there was still hope. The people of Israel would be restored to their land and God's anger toward them for their wickedness and faithlessness would not last forever.

TO THINK ABOUT

The past can't be undone. Yes, God forgives sins, but there are consequences to evil actions. David was forgiven by God, and his eternal destination was not compromised due to his humble and genuine repentance, but there were still consequences of his adultery and murder. David had to suffer those consequences. Presumably Adam and Eve could have repented of their original sin in the Garden of Eden and turned back to God (see Genesis 3), but they had still unleashed the consequences of that sin on the world. Likewise, the sin of Manasseh and other wicked kings, and the people under them, had repercussions for Israel and its people, even though Manasseh repented and after him Josiah was also a good king who repented on behalf of the land, its people, and his forebears. God delayed judgment, but it was still going to come, and come it did during the time of Zedekiah.

It is also true for us that sin and disobedience have consequences. We might ask why there are still consequences of sin if God has forgiven us by the all-sufficient sacrifice of Jesus on our behalf. The answer is that if there is no repercussion for sin or wickedness then evildoers would get away with their actions, and evil and violence would triumph. Judgment must come, and indeed ultimately judgment will come to the world. It is detailed in the later chapters of the prophetic book of Daniel, as well as in the Gospels of Matthew, Mark, and Luke, in 1 and 2 Thessalonians, 2 Peter and most comprehensively in the book of Revelation. God is not indifferent to human suffering, and calls all of us to account for our actions. As an example, if someone who had committed a crime was to turn to Christ, the best counsel would always be to encourage them to give themselves up to the police to take the consequences and to take responsibility for their actions. However, the very good news is that there is hope beyond judgment. Although we do have to take the consequences of our sin and wrongdoing, if we have accepted Christ as Lord, our spiritual debt is paid, our eternal destination is assured, and our suffering for our actions is limited to this world.

Zedekiah's attitude of ignoring God, behaving wickedly, but yet still expecting God to bless him and his nation, is profoundly illogical, however it is surprisingly common. There are many people in the UK who are quick to point out Britain is a Christian nation (in reality it has long since ceased to be so, if indeed it ever was), but yet have no time for God at all. An extreme example of this sort of attitude is held by the likes of the English Defence League and other far-right groups. They will claim Christianity and a sort of crusader-like Anglo-Saxon parody of Christ as part of what they are fighting for, yet their lives and actual beliefs are far removed from anything resembling what it really means to be a Christ-follower. The notion of God and the Christian religion is to them merely a convenient tag which will mean that somehow the nation will be spared judgment and carry God's blessing and support. In the current coronavirus pandemic, many people in wider society are quick to blame a God they may not even believe in and certainly have no time for, but are not willing to consider that God might be speaking through this current situation, and may be trying to get their attention so that they might come to terms with their rebellion against him and come to terms with the fact that they are (as each of us is) fallen sinners in need of God's mercy.

We can feel a little bit sorry for Zedekiah in that he was surely not expecting to become king. He was, after all, behind his brothers Jehoahaz and Jehoiakim in the line of succession. However, events took over, not to mention some serious interference from the Egyptians and the Babylonians, and he was given the job. He also reigned at a time when the fate of his country was all but sealed, meaning his mistakes were amplified perhaps more than the other kings. Plenty before him had done terrible things, but yet hadn't lost the kingdom. However, Zedekiah was very much in the "last chance saloon" from day one. He, like so many before him, was found wanting, but this time it was fatal for the nation. Perhaps Zedekiah was bitter about the situation he had inherited.

Perhaps you, when you read this, also feel that you have been dealt an unfair hand in life. Maybe you didn't have the opportunities others around you had. Perhaps you felt unfairly singled out at school, work, or even by your family. You may have been bullied or ostracized because you were different or because you couldn't or didn't know how to stand up for yourself. You may well be carrying all sorts of bad memories, burdens, and bitterness around with you.

I certainly cannot empathize with everything you may have gone through, although at times I also have played the "it's not fair" or the "if only" card. It is very tempting to do so, but although we may very reasonably have cause to feel aggrieved, can I say that it is a road that goes nowhere except to misery and unhappiness. Can I urge you to try to leave that road. You may need professional help in the form of counselling, and it is no shame to admit you need it. No one should be judging you for that. It might also be that you need to unburden yourself to someone you can trust, who is able to bear and share your pain, and who can walk with you in it and hopefully out of it. I would hope that if you attend a church there would be people there who could be that person of trust, whether it be the pastor, vicar, or another mature Christian in the congregation. This human element is necessary in helping us overcome our inner battles, but I would also urge you to give all your worries, burdens, and hurts to God. Jesus knows what we are going through, and he empathizes with our pain. The emotional, physical, and spiritual suffering he went through in the lead up to and on the cross itself, was beyond anything we will go through. He promised his followers "Come to me, all of you who are weary and carry heavy burdens, and I will give you rest. Take my yoke upon you. Let me teach you, because I am humble and gentle at heart, and you will find rest for your souls. For my yoke is easy to bear, and the burden I give you is light" (Matthew 11:28–30).[1]

1. Some excerpts from a talk given by Paul Barnfield at Hounslow Evangelical Church on the 21 April 2015 have been used in this chapter. My thanks to Paul for his permission to use the talk he gave for this purpose.

Concluding Words

THERE ARE ALL SORTS of other kings who I could have written chapters on, but I think the accounts here give a good overall flavor of the scene in Israel as well as giving us many valuable life lessons. I could have mentioned Uzziah, who was largely good but gave himself the authority to go into the most holy place of the temple, when that was the high priest's right only, and got struck down with leprosy for his troubles. Or Jehoshaphat, who was a man of faith and who God used mightily, yet despite that fact he also made foolish errors in aligning himself to Ahab, Jezebel, and their sons, the consequence of this being that the line of David was almost destroyed. There is also Jotham, who seems to have been consistent in his faith and largely a good king, but who also seems to have been lukewarm, following God himself but refusing to challenge the sinful practices or idols set up in the land. Here we have perhaps a king who was unwilling or fearful to use his God-given authority to ensure a spiritual heritage for his nation. Yes, there is plenty more material, but if you would like to read more about the kings I have missed out, I suggest you read 2 Chronicles and 1 and 2 Kings for yourself, and imagine the scenes set out in those books.

All these kings, whether good or bad, had flaws. Even the godly Josiah was foolish, and paid for it with his life. The other superlative king was of course David, and he exhibited all sorts of flaws in his life. These, as much as the ungodly and wicked kings, serve to remind us that no one is perfect or even close to it. In the book of Romans, the apostle Paul says: "For everyone has sinned;

we all fall short of God's glorious standard" (Romans 3:23). Only Christ came to live the perfect life. In the letter to the Hebrews it says: "This High Priest [Christ] of ours understands our weaknesses, for he faced all of the same testings we do, yet he did not sin" (Hebrews 4:15). Jesus lived the perfect life, he won all his battles with temptation, and so was able to be the perfect sacrifice for our sin, our wrongdoing, our rebellion, one acceptable to God.

There is also hope. The northern kingdom was largely a godless failure, punctuated by short times of comparative success. Unlike the southern kingdom, those in the northern kingdom never resettled their land in an organized way. Whereas Judah returned from exile and rebuilt Jerusalem's walls and temple, those from the northern tribes settled elsewhere or returned to the land to intermingle with other nations. It is thought that the Samaritans of Jesus' time, who the Jews hated, were descended from this intermarriage of those nations with the northern tribes. Yet even in the depths of that once integral part of Israel came a great hope. A lot of pure-born Jews did settle in those lands which had once been given to the tribes of Zebulun and Naphtali, and they were known around the first century AD as Galilee. Into that land Jesus came, and in that area he both preached and lived out the kingdom of God, fulfilling a prophecy made hundreds of years earlier by Isaiah that the people of those lands would see a great light (see Isaiah 9:1). Even in the midst of judgment and despair God can bring hope, light, and life.

If you have never accepted Jesus as your Lord and Savior you can do so any time, simply by asking him into your life and committing yourself to him. The invitation is open, even to the worst of sinners, and those whose lives have been most at odds with God's standard for righteous living. Even the wicked King Manasseh prayed and God answered. That prayer has been recaptured in an apocryphal book called the Prayer of Manasseh, although it is unlikely to have been Manasseh's actual words. Within it are these words: "For the sins I have committed are more in number than the sand of the sea; my transgressions are multiplied, O Lord they are multiplied! . . . And now I bend the knee of my heart, imploring for your kindness" (The Prayer of Manasseh 9a, 11, NRSV).

Today we live in the light of God revealing himself to us in Christ, and we are assured that if we pray to him, asking his forgiveness, he will accept our faith as righteous, and graciously come into our lives. In a vision the apostle John (probably Jesus' closest friend when he walked the earth) has in Revelation 3:20, Jesus says: "Look! I stand at the door and knock. If you hear my voice and open the door, I will come in, and we will share a meal together as friends."

Chronology of Kings

MANY OF THESE DATES and time periods are approximate, as not enough detail is given in the biblical passages. Also, a number of kings seemed to have reigned together as co-regents. For example, Manasseh is only listed here as a reigning between 686 and 642 BC, whereas the biblical narrative says he reigned for fifty-five years. The most likely explanation is that he co-reigned with his father for the last ten to eleven years of Hezekiah's reign.

JUDAH

King	Years (BC)
Rehoboam	931–913
Abijam	913–911
Asa	911–870
Jehoshaphat	870–848
Jehoram	848–841
Ahaziah	841
Athaliah	841–835
Joash	835–796
Amaziah	796–767
Uzziah	767–740
Jotham	740–736
Ahaz	736–729
Hezekiah	729–686
Manasseh	686–642
Amon	642–640
Josiah	640–609
Jehoahaz	609 (3 months)
Jehoiakim	608–598
Jehoiachin	598–597 (3 months)
Zedekiah	597–586

Jerusalem fell in 586 BC.

ISRAEL

King	Years (BC)
Jeroboam I	931–910
Nadab	910–909
Baasha	909–886
Elah	886–885
Zimri	885 (7 days)
Omri	885–874
Ahab	874–853
Ahaziah	853–852
Joram	852–841
Jehu	841–814
Jehoahaz	814–798
Jehoash	798–782
Jeroboam II	782–753
Zechariah	753–752
Shallum	752 (1 month)
Menahem	752–742
Pekahiah	742–740
Pekah	740–732
Hoshea	732–722

Samaria fell in 722 BC.

Bibliography

Gumbel, Nicky. *Questions of Life*. Eastbourne: Kingsway, 1993.
Hudson, J. Francis. *Rabshakeh*. Oxford: Lion, 1992.
Hudson, J. Francis. *Zoheleth*. Oxford: Lion, 1994.
Kendall, R.T. *The Thorn in the Flesh*. London: Hodder and Stoughton, 1999.
Kuhrt, Martin G. *God is Good*. Eugene, OR: Wipf and Stock, 2020.
Psychopaths in Fact and Fiction, "In their own words . . . ". https://www.remorselessfiction.com/criminal-psychopath-quotes.html

Lightning Source UK Ltd.
Milton Keynes UK
UKHW021359291021
393033UK00007B/238